Planes

Paul Stickland

MATHEW PRICE LIMITED

A jumbo jet has landed to pick up passengers and fuel.

It is the largest airliner in the world.

The pilot sits up here. There is a co-pilot and several other crew to help fly the plane.

300 passengers and all their baggage can travel in this jumbo jet. The cabin crew look after them and serve them drinks, snacks and meals.

A JUMBO JET weighs hundreds of tons even without the passengers so the four jet engines have to be very powerful to get the plane off the ground.

PILOT

The UNDERCARRIAGE is lowered for landing but folds back into the body of the plane after it takes off.

First Class

If you are rich you can travel first class. Then you get a big comfortable seat that can convert into a bed and your own TV screen to watch movies or play video games.

The large fuel tanks are hidden in the wings. This plane could fly half way round the world without having to refuel.

Fuel Tanks

Steps

In some airports the planes cannot come right up to the terminal so special steps are driven out to unload the passengers.

Fuel Tanker

refuelling the airplane.

This is a microlight, the very smallest plane in the world. It can be made from a kit at home.

Seaplanes can only take off and land on water.

MICROLIGHTS *are powered by the engine from a motorbike or small car.*

WIRE SUPPORTS

WING

The single wing is made out of special plastic material. It is very strong and light and folds up small when you want to stow it away.

STEEL STRUTS

Microlights can be taken to pieces and put in the back of a pickup truck or SUV.

The cabin will hold six people.

The propellor is driven by a petrol engine. You must always keep out of the way of the propellor when it is spinning or it will hurt you very badly.

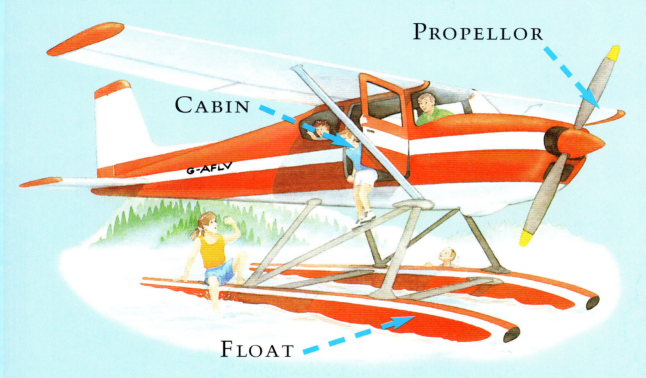

PROPELLOR

CABIN

FLOAT

A SEAPLANE has no wheels. It lands on water on floats filled with air.

In some parts of the world where there are no roads a seaplane can be the only way to travel.

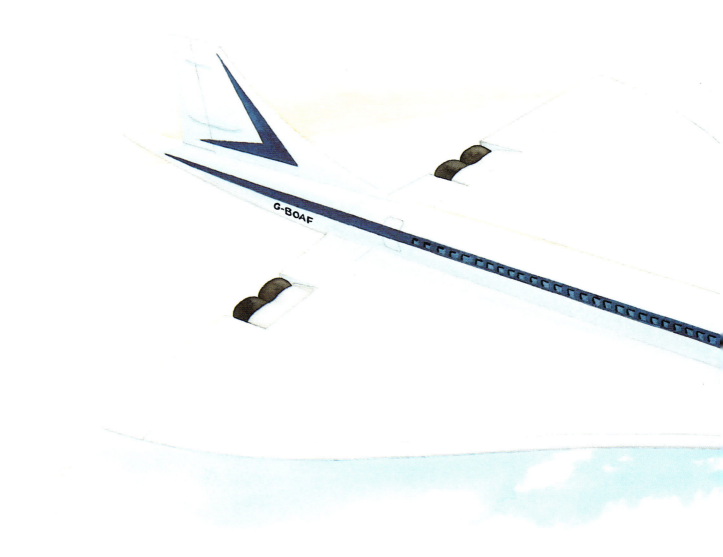

Concorde was the fastest and most advanced airliner in the world.

CONCORDE *was the world's first and only supersonic airliner. It could cross the Atlantic in three hours.*

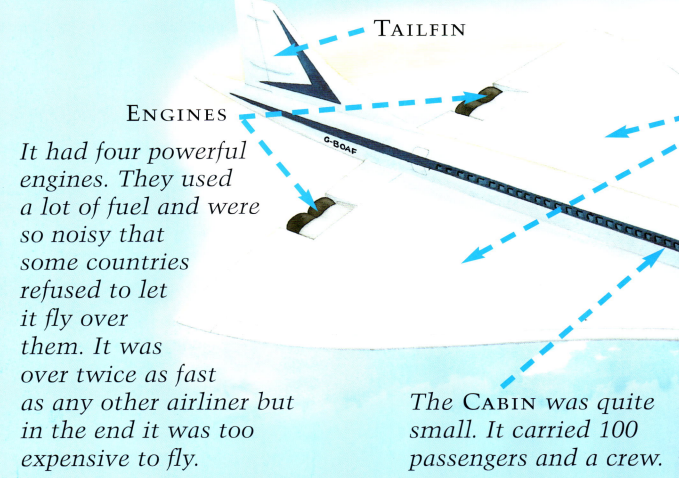

TAILFIN

ENGINES

It had four powerful engines. They used a lot of fuel and were so noisy that some countries refused to let it fly over them. It was over twice as fast as any other airliner but in the end it was too expensive to fly.

The CABIN *was quite small. It carried 100 passengers and a crew.*

CONCORDE *had a cruising speed of twice the speed of sound. That's faster than a speeding bullet. It went 23 miles in a minute.*

Concorde had no tailplane. It had large delta wings and a tailfin instead.

It cruised at 60,000 feet, eleven miles above the earth.

Delta Wings

Nose Cone

To fly so fast Concorde had to be a smooth pointed shape. The very sharp nose could be lowered during take-off and landing.

Come flying in an old-fashioned bi-plane. You can get very cold so don't forget your scarf and goggles.

This twin-engine plane can take off from a very short runway, a field or even a beach.

A BI-PLANE has two wings. This is an old one. It has no modern instruments so the pilot would look over the side and follow roads or rivers.

It has no cabins and no windows.

SCARF for keeping warm.

GOGGLES to protect your eyes from insects and the force of the wind.

The pilot isn't using a wheel to steer with, he is using a JOYSTICK.

Modern airplanes can retract their wheels. These are fixed in one position.

This is a TWIN-ENGINED PLANE. Many parts of the world do not have airports with proper runways. As long as there is a strip of smooth ground 100 metres long, this plane can land and take off again. A jumbo jet would need a mile of runway.

FLAPS, two on each wing, give greater control.

It is used for flying in emergency medical supplies or as a flying ambulance.

In some places it is a taxi. It is nicknamed a puddle jumper because it is often used to fly from island to island.

A glider has no engine, so it has to be towed up into the air to get it going. Then the little plane goes back down and the glider flies silently through the skies.

Once it is high in the sky the tow rope is dropped and the pilot glides silently down to earth. Even though he has no engine he can go up as well as down by riding air currents. They can even loop the loop.

WINGS
In order to ride the air a glider has very long thin wings.

AILERONS – for pointing the nose up or down.

Very light **FUSELAGE**

HANGARS for housing small planes.

HANG GLIDER

Every plane has its own NUMBER

RUDDER *for steering the aeroplane.*

COCKPIT
There is only room for one person. If the pilot has to bale out, he is wearing a parachute so he can float safely down to earth.

On landing the wings and tail are taken off and the whole plane can be put in a trailer and towed home by car.

The How, Why, What For Page

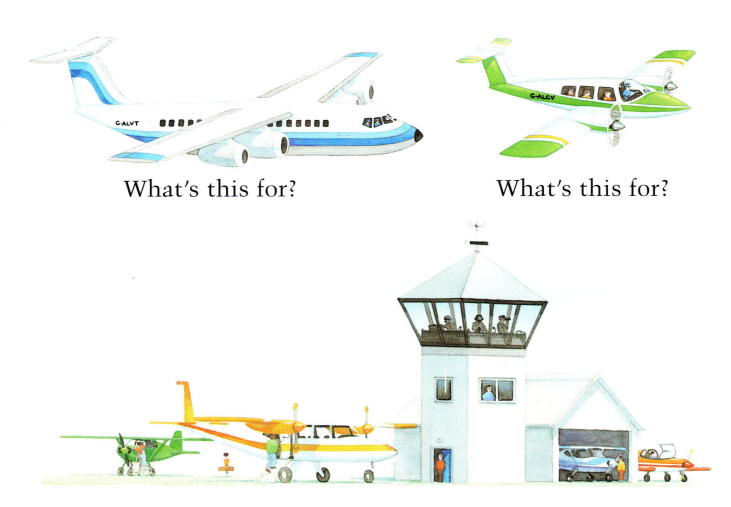

What's this for?

What's this for?

What's this tower for?

Why are there two pilots?   What's that thing on a pole for?

What's this for?   What kind of plane is this?

The **Answers** Page

It's a small jet plane, for carrying 80 passsengers.

It's a training plane. Both the instructor and the trainee pilot have a set of controls.

It's a far smaller plane, for carrying six passengers. Instead of jet engines it has twin propellers.

It's a windsock. It shows pilots the strength and direction of the wind. Planes need to take off and land into the wind.

It's the control tower. Every airport has to have one to help pilots land and take off safely.

It's just for fun!

It's used for aerobatics. This one is part of the Red Arrows aerobatics team. It's for stunts and tricks such as flying upside down in close formation and looping the loop.

Copyright © Paul Stickland 1992, 2004
This edition first published in the UK 2004
by Mathew Price Limited
The Old Glove Factory, Bristol Road
Sherborne, Dorset DT9 4HP, UK

Designed by Douglas Martin
All rights reserved
Printed in China
ISBN 1-84248-116-9